Grade 1 Piano

CW00672348

Improve your sight-reading!

Paul Harris

Contents

FABER *ff* MUSIC

Practice chart

	Comments (from you, your teacher or parent)	Done!
Stage 1		
Stage 2		
Stage 3		
Stage 4		
Stage 5		

Teacher's name _____

Telephone _____

© 2013 by Faber Music Ltd
This edition first published in 2013
Bloomsbury House 74-77 Great Russell Street London WC1B 3DA
Music processed by MacMusic
Cover and page design by Susan Clarke
Printed in England by Caligraving Ltd
All rights reserved

ISBN 10: 0-571-53751-0
EAN13: 978-0-571-53751-8

To buy Faber Music publications or to find out about the full range of titles available
please contact your local music retailer or Faber Music sales enquiries:
Faber Music Ltd, Burnt Mill, Elizabeth Way, Harlow CM20 2HX
Tel: +44 (0) 1279 82 89 82 Fax: +44 (0) 1279 82 89 83
sales@fabermusic.com fabermusicstore.com

Introduction

Being a good sight-reader is so important and it needn't be difficult! If you work through this book carefully – always making sure that you really understand each exercise before you play it you'll never have problems learning new pieces or doing well at sight-reading in exams!

Using the workbook

1 Rhythmic exercises

Make sure you have grasped these fully before you go on to the melodic exercises: it is vital that you really know how the rhythms work. There are a number of ways to do the exercises, several of which are outlined in Stage 1. Try them all out. Can you think of more ways to do them?

2 Melodic exercises

These exercises use just the notes and rhythms for the Stage, and also give some help with fingering. If you want to sight-read fluently and accurately, get into the simple habit of working through each exercise in the following ways before you begin to play it:

- Make sure you understand the rhythm and counting. Clap the exercise through.
- Look at the shape of the tune, particularly the highest and lowest notes. Which finger do you need to start on to be able to play it? The exercises have this fingering added to get you started.
- Try to hear the piece through in your head. Always play the first note to help.

3 Prepared pieces

Work your way through the questions first, as these will help you to think about or 'prepare' the piece. Don't begin playing until you are pretty sure you know exactly how the piece goes.

4 Going solo!

It is now up to you to discover the clues in this series of practice pieces. Give yourself about a minute and do your best to understand the piece before you play. Check the rhythms and hand position, and try to hear the piece in your head.

Always remember to feel the pulse and to keep going steadily once you've begun. Good luck and happy sight-reading!

Terminology:
Bar = measure

Stage 1

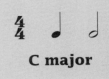

Rhythmic exercises

Always vary the way you do the rhythmic exercises. Here are a few ideas:
- Tap the pulse with your right foot (sometimes use your left foot!) and clap the rhythm.
- Tap the pulse with one hand and the rhythm with the other (swap hands!).
- Tap the pulse with your foot and play the rhythm on a single note (either hand).
- Tap the pulse with your foot and make up a simple tune to fit the rhythm.

Before you begin each exercise count two bars in; the first out loud and the second silently.

4   Now write your own exercise and then clap it.

Melodic exercises

Set 1: Right hand

Before playing this first melodic exercise, write down the rhythm on
the line underneath. The first bar is done for you. Then clap it.

Set 2: Left hand

Set 3: Both hands, with phrasing

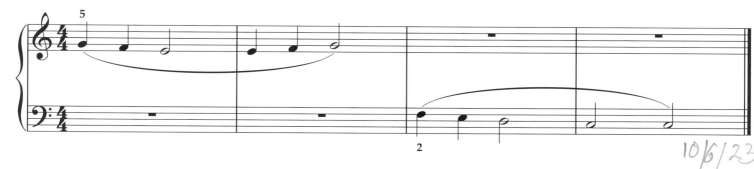

10/6/23

Prepared pieces

1 How many beats are there in each bar? What will you count?

2 What is the key? Play the scale (or microscale*).

3 Look for the highest and lowest notes in each hand and check your fingering.

4 Can you spot any repeated patterns – rhythmic or melodic?

5 How will you put character into this piece?

6 Try to hear the music (melody and rhythm) in your head before you begin.

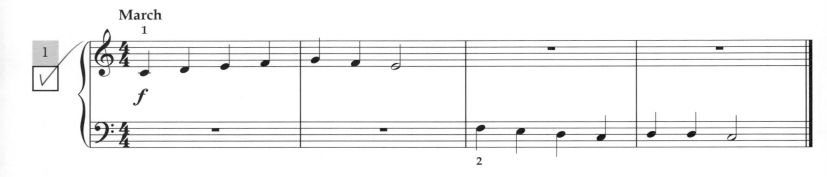

1 How will you count this piece?

2 Tap the rhythm then hear the rhythm silently in your head.

3 What is the key? Play the scale (or microscale).

4 Can you spot any repeated patterns – rhythmic or melodic?

5 How will you put character into this piece?

6 Try to hear the music in your head.

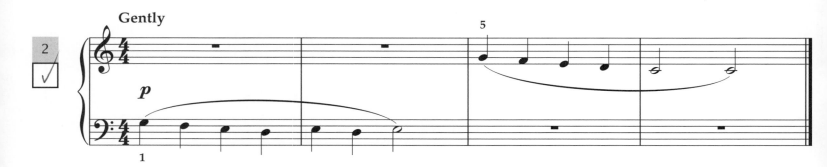

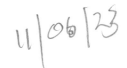

* See page 24 for details.

Going solo!

Remember to prepare each piece carefully before you play it.

11/06/23

Stage 2

Rhythmic exercises

Remember to count two bars in!

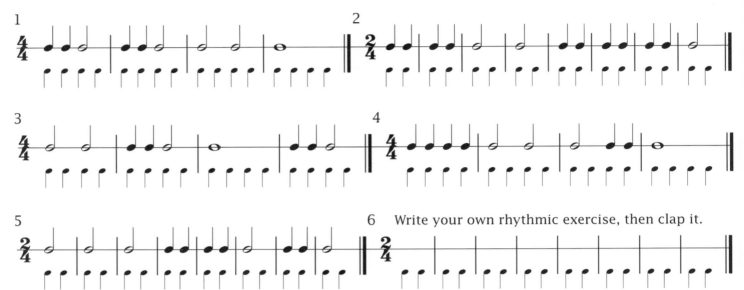

Melodic exercises

Set 1: Introducing leaps of a third

Set 2: Leaps of a fourth

Set 3: Leaps of a fifth

13/6/23

Prepared pieces

> 1 How many beats is each ♩ worth?
>
> 2 What will you count? Tap the rhythm of the piece. Now hear the rhythm in your head.
>
> 3 What is the key? Play the scale (or microscale).
>
> 4 Can you spot any repeated patterns – rhythmic or melodic?
>
> 5 How will you put character into this piece?
>
> 6 Try to hear the music in your head before you begin.

Skipping

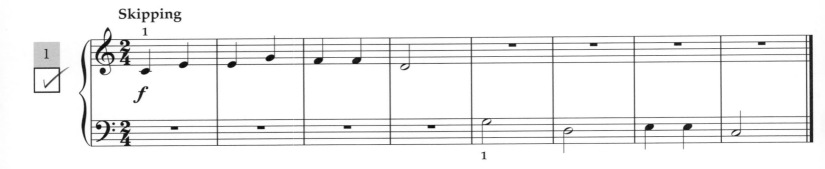

> 1 How many beats is the 𝅝 worth?
>
> 2 Say the letter names of each note. Play the scale (or microscale).
>
> 3 Look for the highest and lowest notes and check your fingering.
>
> 4 Can you spot the leaps of a third and fourth?
>
> 5 How will you put character into this piece?
>
> 6 Try to hear the music in your head before you begin.

Calmly

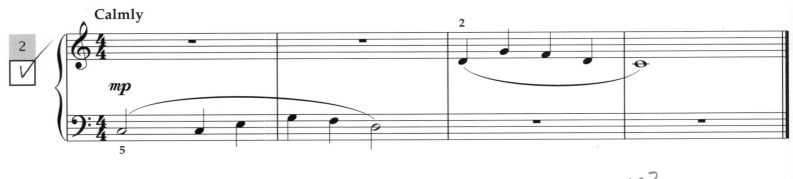

14/06/23

Going solo!

Remember to prepare each piece carefully before you play it.

16/6/23 + 4/9/23

Stage 3

Rhythmic exercises

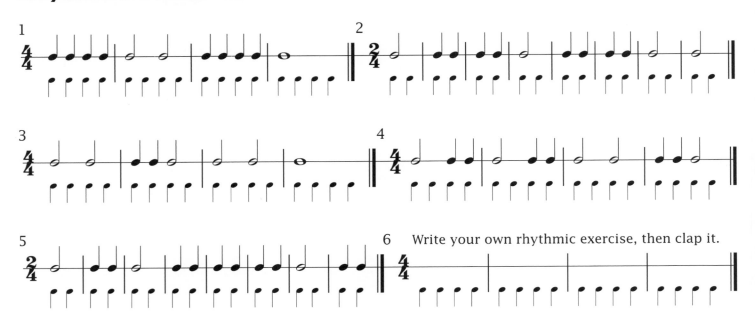

Melodic exercises

Set 1: Introducing G major

20/6/23

Set 2: Introducing simple hands together

Set 3: More hands together

20/6/23

Prepared pieces

> 1 What is the key of this piece? Play the scale (or microscale).
>
> 2 What will you count? Tap the rhythm of the piece. Now hear the rhythm in your head.
>
> 3 Think about your hand position and place your hands over the correct keys.
>
> 4 Can you spot any repeated patterns – rhythmic or melodic?
>
> 5 How will you put character into this piece?
>
> 6 Try to hear the music in your head before you begin.

March time

> 1 What will you count? Tap the rhythm of the piece. Now hear the rhythm in your head.
>
> 2 What is the key? Play the scale (or microscale).
>
> 3 What do you notice about the final two bars?
>
> 4 What pattern do the three notes in bar 1 form?
>
> 5 How will you put character into this piece?
>
> 6 Try to hear the music in your head before you begin.

Allegro

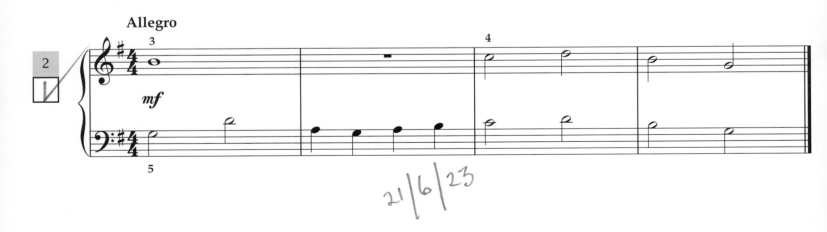

21/6/23

Going solo!

Remember to prepare each piece carefully before you play it.

23/6/23

Stage 4

Rhythmic exercises

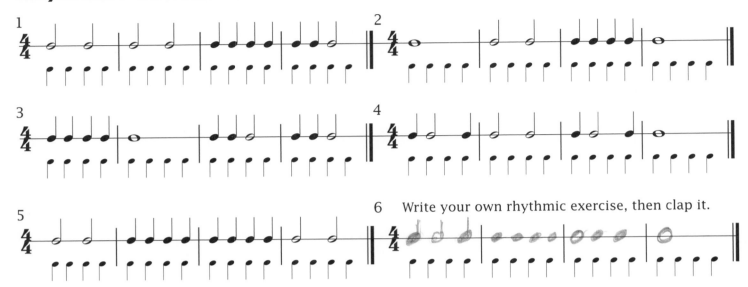

6 Write your own rhythmic exercise, then clap it.

Melodic exercises

As you get to the end of a phrase make sure that you are looking
ahead to see what comes next – notes and rhythm.

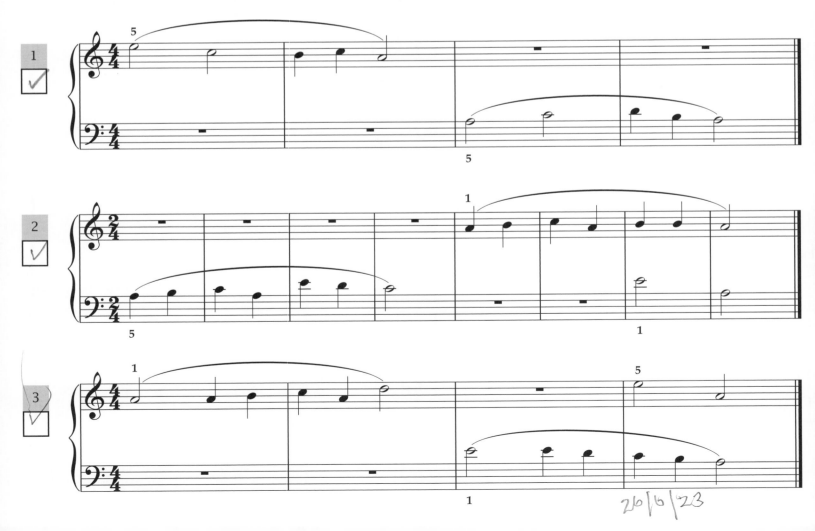

26/6/'23

27/8/23

Prepared pieces

1 What is the key of this piece? Play the scale (or microscale) in both hands.

2 Say the names of all the notes. Where is the biggest leap?

3 What will you count? Tap the rhythm of the piece. Now hear the rhythm in your head.

4 Look for the highest and lowest notes and check your fingering.

5 How will you put character into this piece?

6 Try to hear the music in your head before you begin.

I've just had an idea!

1

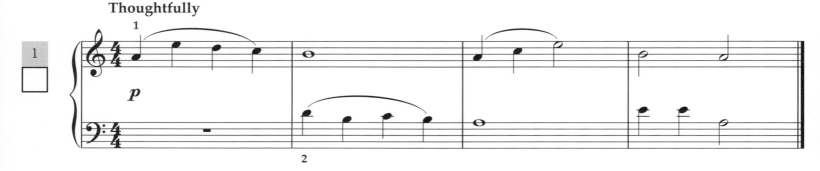

1 What is the key of this piece? Play the scale (or microscale) in both hands.

2 How many intervals of a third can you spot?

3 Say the names of all the notes. Where is the biggest leap?

4 What will you count? Tap the rhythm of the piece. Now hear the rhythm in your head.

5 How will you put character into this piece?

6 Try to hear the music in your head before you begin.

Chit chat

2

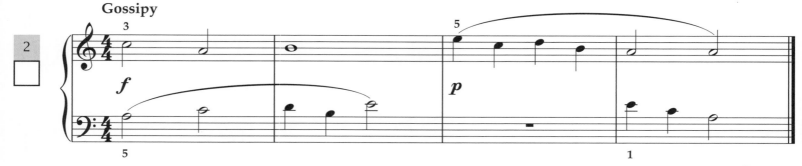

29/6/23

Going solo!

Remember to prepare each piece carefully before you play it.

29/6/23

Stage 5

Rhythmic exercises

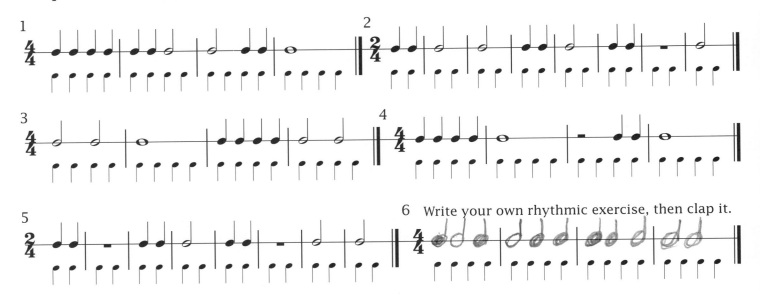

6 Write your own rhythmic exercise, then clap it.

Melodic exercises

In these exercises your hands may be over different notes. Check
the fingering and your hand position carefully before you begin!

Set 1: C major new hand positions

30/6/23

Set 2: G major

Check whether your finger is over the black key before you begin!

Set 3: A minor

Prepared pieces

> **1** How many beats are there in each bar?
>
> **2** What is the key of this piece? Play the scale (or microscale).
>
> **3** Find the correct position for both hands. Do you need to play a black key?
>
> **4** Can you spot any repeated patterns – rhythmic or melodic?
>
> **5** How will you put character into this piece?
>
> **6** Hear the piece in your head before you begin.

Pass the pepper pot please

> **1** How will you count this piece?
>
> **2** What is the key of this piece? Play the scale (or microscale).
>
> **3** Tap the rhythm of this piece then hear the rhythm silently in your head.
>
> **4** Can you spot any repeated patterns – rhythmic or melodic?
>
> **5** How will you put character into this piece?
>
> **6** Hear the piece (melody and rhythm) through in your head.

With a pinch of salt

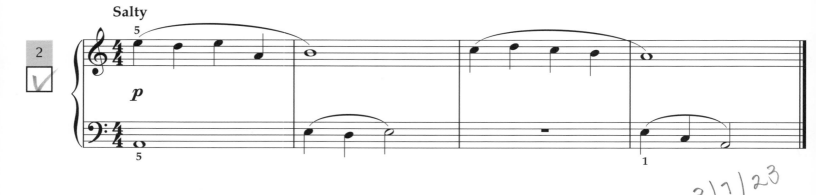

3/7/23

Going solo!

Remember to prepare each piece carefully before you play it.

Taking the snake for a slither

Taking the dog for a walk

Taking the mouse for a scurry

Taking the kangaroo for a hop

Taking the sloth for a nap

The golden rules

A sight-reading checklist

Before you begin to play a piece at sight, always consider the following:

1 Look at the time signature and decide how you will count the piece.

2 Look at the key signature and find the notes which need raising or lowering.

3 Notice patterns – especially those based on scales and arpeggios.

4 Check the fingering and position for each hand.

5 Notice any markings that will help you convey the character.

6 Count at least two bars in.

When performing a sight-reading piece

1 Keep feeling the pulse.

2 Keep going at a steady tempo.

3 Ignore mistakes.

4 Look ahead – at least to the next note.

5 Keep your hands in position on the keyboard.

6 Play musically, always trying to convey the character of the music.

Look at each piece for about half a minute and try to feel that you are understanding what you see (just like reading these words).

Don't begin until you think you are going to play the piece accurately.

Microscales
If you don't know the whole scale, just the first five notes or even just
the first three notes will do! Both patterns will give a good feel of the key.

 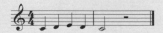